# PRISON WRITERS

An anthology collected by

## Tom Hadaway

Sirkka Liisa Konttinen

Second Print 1987

First published 1986 by IRON PRESS
5 Marden Terrace, Cullercoats
North Shields, Tyne & Wear NE30 4PD
Tel: Tyneside (091) 2531901

Printed by Tyneside Free Press Workshop
5 Charlotte Sq
Newcastle upon Tyne

Typeset by True North
Cover design by Irene Reddish
**Book Paste-up by Norman Davison**
Inside photographs by
Sirkka Liisa Konttinen

ISBN 0 906228 25 5

*IRON Press books represented by*
*Password Books Ltd*
*25 Horsell Rd*
*London N1 1XL*
*Tel 01-607-1154*


*Front cover lettering by Sally Brown*

## ACKNOWLEDGEMENT

For his prison residency Tom Hadaway is indebted to Ms Lucie
Milton, and the Artist's Agency, for the sponsorship.

# The Writer in Prison

THREE DAYS A WEEK FOR TWELVE WEEKS, TOM HADAWAY WORKED IN HM PRISONS OF DURHAM, FRANKLAND, AND LOW NEWTON, TO ENCOURAGE, AND ADVISE PRISONERS IN THEIR WRITING.

# Acknowledgement

While drawing attention to the limitations imposed by prison rule, the Governors and Educational Chief Officers of these prisons, encouraged this project in a very fair, and supportive manner, for which I thank them.

Thank you to the men and women, on the wrong side of the bars. Prisons have a cruel and despairing side to them, and it would be fitting if they were the means of explaining where 'we' have all gone wrong.

Tom Hadaway

*The photographs for this book, by Sirkka Liisa Konttinen were taken at Low Newton prison. Permission to take photographs at Durham Prison was refused.*

# INTRODUCTION

"Do I look the sort of woman who would murder her husband?", *she said, by way of an opening remark.*
*Entering the confine of her cell, maybe she was offering me reassurance.*
*There were three male prisons, plus two female enclaves. Ages spanned eighteen to seventy years, and they came from Colombia to Gateshead, County Galway, to County Cleveland.*
"I want to write my life story", *she continued,* "So how do I begin?".
*How about, 'Do I look the sort of woman who would murder her husband?''.*
*But recollection was too painful, and on her locker, the beautiful children in the photograph stared wistfully, and sadly down. Anyhow, her solicitor forbid the activity, fearing prosecution access to the material.*
*Within the prison, the prisoner, within the prisoner, the imprisoned memory.*
*But there were other doors, locked, and barred.*
"There is no point in our writing anything, so why write?"
*The tattooed, young man was being polite. I was lucky! He could as easily have told me to piss off, so vibrant his aggression, and resentment. Strangely, he had articulated my first proposition, about there being little point in writing unless you had something to say.*
*The population of Durham prison is about the same as a large secondary modern school. Going with the pretention of stimulating creative writing, what can you expect? The mixture is the same, some very intelligent young men, some not. But, take any thousand people off the streets of Tyneside, or High Wycombe, how many potential major poets, novelists, and dramatists will be among them? It was not the point of the exercise.*
*But consider the pretention of liberal education, that it has been freely available, offering opportunity to all, and it was simply up to the individual....*
"Bullshit!" *The tattooed, young prisoner ran out of politeness, and he was right. So, maybe ten per cent of working class lads pass the exams, and go on to further education, and the cultural.inheritance, but what of the rest?*
"Haven't done your homework, have you boy?" "What's the matter with you?" "Wasting your time, and mine", "Are you listening to me" "You lazy little..."
*Filled with reproach, and rejection, their schooldays are not unlike a prison sentence, and the fault they are told, lies within themselves.*
"You've had your chance, and you've blown it".
*Inexorably, all they acquire, is a massive lack of confidence. The gutsy ones might run away, the weak slide into self abnegation.*
"There is no point in our writing anything".
*Now prison adds to the tattooed, young man's conviction of his own worthlessness.*
*Open that door, in twelve weeks!*

## Tom Hadaway

1

# Nothing will Come of What We Write

FIVE VOICES OF TEENAGE PRISONERS
IN REMEDIAL CLASS ONE. LOW NEWTON.

Nothing will come of what we write
So why write?

Freedom is what's important,
Freedom is important to me too,
And to everyone here.

Family is important,
Friends are important,
You've no friends in jail,
You can only trust your brothers, cousins.
You can't even trust them.

Money is important,
That's why you commit crimes,
That's one reason anyway.

It's for your food, clothes, and drink,
But being let down is the worst,

You get funny dreams in here,
It seems like something is on my face,
Making me take deep breaths,
and then I go out.

It's important to keep your mind blank, and that's difficult.

Every night I'm lying in bed,
Thinking about my kid,
It upsets me.

**By courtesy of Peter**

# Why Write

Why should I write, I don't know,
Just somewhere for my thoughts to go.

Write of woman, family, friends,
Write to please my biro pen.

Write for freedom in my brain,
Never want to see prison again.

Write of love, I had, and lost,
Write of how much it all has cost.

I am lonely, write of that,
Can't keep it all beneath my hat.

Write of home, for which I long,
I'd be there now, but I did wrong.

**Stuart Watson – LOW NEWTON**

# Help Me

Help me, someone, help me,
For my life is slipping by,
I'm locked up here in prison,
And left alone to cry.

The pain that I am suffering,
Is much more than I can bare,
Help me someone help me,
Please tell me what to do.

Please say that you can help me,
'Cos I'm me, and I am real,
Help me, someone help me,
My name is David Beal.

**David Beal – DURHAM**

3

*"We sat in the depressing formality of desks, and hard chairs, the classroom architecture of yesterday, in which we had failed, and which had failed us'.*

*Older now, and shabbier, and unrelieved,except for a faint March sunlight, offering through mesh, and bars its thin compassion to yesterdays children."*

*T.H.*

# The Lonely House

We're in the 'Lonely House',
We're lonely here.
With our long forgotten dreams,
It's such fun, yeah, it's such fun,
With your love in a void,
Like little orphans in the home,
With nowhere to call their own,
We're lonely here in the 'Lonely House'.
It's not them, no not them,
But they'er so numb,
And we're so dumb,
That's why we have no keys,
Just pityful please,
I'd like to get to know you,
Your deodorant smells nice,
Rinse your mouth with Listerine,
Blow disenfectant in my eyes,
They are germ free adolescence,
Cleanliness is their obsession.
Cleans their teeth ten times a day,
Scrub away the SR way.
Counting the days, counting the nights.
Convicted, remanded, all are we,
Living together happily,
We are all in the Nick together,
In the 'Lonely House'.

## Tracie Simpson – LOW NEWTON

4

# To Let

One bed apartments,
Set in it's own grounds,
Communal entrance hall,
and landings,
Comprises, all amenities,
Bed, breakfast, lunch, evening meal,
Inclusive with hot, cold water, central heating.
Has it's own village shop, and post office.
Further enquiries,
nearest Police Station,
To be 'fitted up', and recommended.
No references required.
Antecedants are an advantage.
No deposit on vacation.
Short, long term lease,
Depending on conviction,
Open to offers!

**Olly Sweeney – LOW NEWTON**

# Prediction

There is a feeling that won't go away,
You are branded a thief until the end of your day
You commit a crime, get sent to jail,
If you've got a record, there's no chance of bail.
They ask why you done it, "For money", you reply,
But they give you dole money, and expect you to get by.
I can't live on dole money, and Thatcher don't care,
When taxes are collected she gets her share,
Where will she be when the bombs drop around,
In a special shelter under the ground,
There'll be another war, I'll guarantee,
But no place to run for you and me, .
So forget what you've planned for your life ahead,
'Cos in less than five years, we will all be dead.

**Muir – Redcar – LOW NEWTON**

6

# There are Moments

There are moments,
So painful in their truth,
They tear at me,
Pull at my very existence,
I survive them,
With scars,
That heal,
For you.

There are mornings,
That lie in our future,
I feel them,
They are real within me,
I treasure them,
Keep them,
Save them,
For you.

There are months,
That pass like years,
I live them,
They weigh like stones,
I carry them,
Bear them,
Silently,
For you.

There are memories,
That I could hide within,
If I choose,
I could close myself away,
No-one would know,
Or care,
Except,
For you.

David – FRANKLAND

7

*"Who looks after the baby while you are in here?"*
"Me mam!"
*Not married!*
"No".
*"Does it worry you?"*
"Money is what worries me. Not havin' any. Where I live, it's another world. No chance a job that'll bring in enough to pay your way, y'know! Baby clothes, everythin! Ye probably think A just go graftin' for kicks, well A do a bit like!
But if A didn't go graftin' A couldn't get by.
*How old are you?*
Nineteen!

# LOW NEWTON

*"Why write? Well, it is only a way of recording experience. Sure some do it better than others. Some on an ego trip, some for the hell of it, or it's a nice way to earn a living.*
*But it's no-ones exclusive right, anymore than painting, or music. What matters is the experience. What informs is the experience. Not the prose, but the real life experience, liberated and freely expressed. Your experience! That is what is important. Yes, important, because you are important. Well, if they didn't tell you that at school, they must have forgotten."*

*T.H.*

# 'Grafting'

Note. Grafting     – Shoplifting
    To skelp     – A short sharp shock
    On the bash – Prostitution
    Hoist     – The proceeds of shoplifting
    Cowies     – Older women
    Gadgies     – Older men
    Muskers     – Store detectives
    Cushty     – Faint hearted
    Scran     – Food
    Clammin'     – Hungry

"Minnie, open the door. Mick'll be here in a minute".
"My God, nine in the mornin', what's ya game?
A thought yous wasn't ganin' graftin'"
"Giz quarter an' hour, and A'll be ready. Can't die in peace these days."
The car horn was tootin' fifty to the dozen outside. Still half asleep, I joined the other lasses at the bottom of the terrace, and waited for Mick turnin' round.
"Eee luv, i's bloody freezin'. A only hope Mick's got that heater fixed".

"Who! ye's lot! What ye standin' aboot for, get yor arses in here, there's money ti make".

The way he says that makes me cringe, ye'd think we were on the bash, the way he puts it over.

"Well girls! where will we park today??"

"Doon by Olivers, as we want ti skelp Fen's first".

As we're walking up to Fenwicks, we see another team of grafters with a bag of hoist.

"Hope ye's lot haven't been on wor pitch!"

"Nee chance, ye want ti see the cowies in there noo. The size o' them, an elly ain't gorra look in, an' gadgies an' all."

"Makes no odds what size, if yor quick enough, the' divven give ye a second look".

"Howway ye's lot, we've got work ti do".


But mind, A wouldn't like one o' them gorillas puttin' thor hands on my shoulders. I'd pass oot on the spot, nee sweat.

"Howway then".

Inside Fen's we go, to wor favourite spot, loads of cover.

"Get that bin liner oot".

"Howway then, stock us up. Not too much! I ain't ganna carry the sodden thing oot only ti have it bust open".

"O.K. Watch me back, in case thor's muskers on me tail. Low Newtons the last place A wanna gan."

"Gan on man! Ya as soond as a poond".

"Ya sure?"

"Course I am ya cushty! Micks outside in case of owt happens".


"Ye knaa what gets me, ye bring a man in case oot happens, but when it comes ti the crunch, it's us lasses who have all the bottle. Anyway, let's take the gear back to the motor, and gan for a scran, 'cos A'm clammin!"

"Aye! so am I. Only had a piece o' toast this mornin'".

"There's Mick over there. 'Wo' ye! What ye think yor doin'? Divven think for one minute yor ganna get any wages from us. Yor supposed ti wait outside the shop, not keep toot on Greys Monument. Bloody useless!"

"Well, for my money, I'd rather gan yem, as I've got this funny feeling".

"Howway man! Let's have this scran first".

As we are walking up to Olivers a crowd has gathered outside Fen's. Bizzys all over the place. Anyhow we walk away, not all that concerned about what's going on in the background, until I hear a woman shouting.

"Over there! There they are!"

Like I said, Low Newton's the last place I wanted to gan.

# Marie Dinning – FEMALE WING, LOW NEWTON

# Child to Woman

They put me in prison,
When only a child,
So why are they shocked
I grew up so wild?
There was only sentence
Could be given to me.
I was too young for life.
So I got H.M.P.

Now I'm in Durham at her
      Majesty's pleasure,
Is it ten years, fifteen, or
      maybe forever?

I know I deserve it,
As I killed with a knife,
But just how much more
Do they want of my Life?
They say in three years,
You'll have another review,
To see if you've changed,
We want a new you.

How can I change?
What do I know?
I've spent seven years,
Behind this locked door,
I'll try my best, do all I can,
One thing I do know,
I've changed from the (wild) child,'
To a bitter woman.

## Laura Greenwood – 'H' WING, DURHAM

*I'd asked for an audience, so on my first night in Durham, they shamelessly stuffed sixty, hardened, academic failures into a twenty foot square room, and invited me to be eaten alive. Just as shamelessly I played the gallery.*

*"We" are the victims. In a society that values property more than it values people, there are two kinds of education. The kind they keep for themselves, and the kind they give to 'us'. Resigned to underachievement, we give up believing in our creative potential, and 'they' take over the libraries, the books, the theatres, the art galleries..."*

*In the corridor, the 'screw' nervously folded away his 'Daily Mirror'.*

*"But there is another kind of education, and it's the kind you get for yourself, and for the likes of us, maybe it's the only kind that matters".*

*I was quoting from my play 'The Filleting Machine', but I have every right to believe this. That the committed burglar also valued property more than he valued people was something we could sort out later.*

*"What do you want us to write about", they cried.*

*"Yourselves!"*

*Subsequently, eight of them turned up for the creative writing class.*

T.H.

# Death

A gun could not shoot me,
A stone could not bruise me,
A name could not harm me,
For I am not here.
Yet I come to receive you, hold you,
And comfort you,
But you cannot hear that I am here,
And now I am gone, and you come too.

## G. Phillips – LOW NEWTON

# Testimony

I am sitting here these walls so gray,
Thinking of my freedom day,
I thought two years would have learned me so,
But from right, and wrong I'll never know,
Understand when I apologise,
I am not telling you lies,
Awake at night, thinking all this crime,

'Only makes me do more time,
Time that makes me violent, and all I do is shout,
But shouting to a crowd that's deaf, nothing comes out,
So I remain violent, and keep my pride,
'Cos when you're in here there's no where to hide.

Muir-Redcar – LOW NEWTON

# Heroin

Sitting in my cell,
Wondering what the hell
Without any smack,
The pains in my back,
Withdrawing again,
It's always the same,
the people I love,
Have given me the shove
God, I wish the pain would go.

Inside these four walls,
Things creep, and crawl,
Out of my mind,
People so unkind,
All alone,
My only wish is to go home,
I won't do it again,
But then,
I always say the same.

M. Dinning – LOW NEWTON

# Even the Stars are Dead

Freedom is an easily spoken word,
But facts are stubborn things,
That will not brush away,

Consider these, for we have condemned them,
Whence the mockery, whence the tears,
Tomorrow has no hand in their future,
Tomorrow only the discovery of self,
Tomorrow the conscious acceptance of guilt.
Darkness opens like a knife for you,
You who bloom when danger's all around,
You who's mind orbits in a different groove.
You who long for freedom,
How can I warn, how can I spare,
You of the future, who's face is my own,?
Who's treading down alleys I have trod,
How can I scare you, put you off,
Mugging, and murdering, running ever faster,
Toward the dark abyss of ultimate crime?

Oh' but that's been going on since time began,
How can I put into words that dark anguish?

Just round the corner where you will find,
Mass production of twisted thoughts,
Hollow laughter, endless tears, a fortress against ideas,
Where only the stars seem friendly,

Oh' but that's been going on since the world began,
It's better that you should go quickly,
If this is your goal, this your ultimate self,
Rip the edge off your ideal, your dream,
For you,
         Even the stars are dead.

# A 'Lifer' for Murder Category a. – H WING FEMALE

*A prisoners desire for anonymity or the requirements of the Home Office in security
means the withholding of some names.*

*I understood she had arrived a girl of seventeen, unable to speak English.*

*The classic features, and intense, rapid speech, demanded attention, but when she
recalled the chaos of her own land, the battles, the engagements, she spoke dispassion-*

13

*ately, matter of fact, in the manner of a veteran soldier.*
  *She apologised for her writing being clumsy, childlike. She was now twenty five, and*
*had been in prison for nearly eight years.*

*T.H.*

# I was Waking to a Memory of Lebanon and Home

Yes, well . . . I might as well, get out of bed,
since I can't get back to sleep.

I've got this crazy feeling, to slip out of the house,
and on the pavement put on my shoes.

No soul in sight. Just what I like.

One step, two step, then wild I be, and fast I run,
I don't have to go very far.

I reach, and I climb the pine tree, then sit on a branch
and for a minute I rest.

The early morning songs of the birds I hear. I feel so
good, so proud, and round my throne I look.

Glance back, I see from so far away the sky embracing
the Mediteranian sea. Peaceful village to the left, a
castle to the right.

A long road, and in the house my family still asleep.


From the fig tree, my pyjama pockets I filled. Twice I wiped with my sleeves,
and ate two of these.

Glad my mother didn't see me, or another telling off I'd
have undergone. Now off my shoes I take, and back into
the house I sneak.

14

My sister caught me, but she promised not of this to speak,
... if I take her next time with me.

We emptied the figs from my pocket to a bowl, and hid it
at the bottom of the fridge.

My brother woke up, looked crossly at me, then about where
I were, he asked.

No-where but in bed, I said, but couldn't help but laugh
while I speak.

"Your pyjamas is a mess", he said.

I say, "Now this door is locked, and no balcony to go out
to, no fields, no trees".

But I got this crazy feeling it's dawn still, so I better get back to sleep.

# Klhoud – H WING DURHAM

Mrs H.
Probation Officer
c/o H.M Prison,
Styall

Dear Mrs. H,
    Regardless of what you say, I am losing my little one ... it is destroying me each day
thinking of what is happening to my baby. I love my children regardless of what I have
done. How do you know how my children will react seeing me in here. . . . I have a letter
from Rachel that to me has no feeling of love in it ...

*H. WING is an integral part of Durham prison housing 36 female prisoners in a high
security wing. It seemed to me that they endured prison life with equanimity not
found in the male prison. They were cheerful, friendly, and outgoing. Which is why they
had the extra security fence.*
    *But for women the cost of imprisonment is greater.*

15

# The Vicious Circle

I was put into care when I was three, and a half, but always wondered where my mother, and father were, and why they weren't looking for me.

When I was sixteen, I'd given up hope of ever knowing who they were, when this happened. I was working in a hostel run by nuns in Glasgow. Old people, and travellers came in for a rest, and a cup of tea. I got on talking with this old lady about where she came from, and I told her about the troubles I'd been in. "Donachie?", she said, "Is that your name?"

"That's right', I said, "Bridget Donachie".

"Would ye know an Annie Donachie", she said, and I remembered I'd had a sister of that name.

"Well love, I'm your grandmother", the old lady told me. She directed me to my family who were living on a site near Manchester, and that's how I got back to them.

But I never forgive my mother for not fighting for me. When she died, I was the only one who didn't cry at the funeral. She said, because of what she'd done, they'd declared her not to be a fit parent, but I felt if she had really loved me, she would have fought for me.

Now I'm in the same trouble. My two youngest kids are fostered while I'm in here, and they never write. I don't know if they are getting my letters, and I don't even know the name, and address of where they are fostered. My probation officer won't tell me, she says she can't. Can you tell me what I should do. I don't want my kids to grow up thinking about me the way I thought about my mother.

## BRIDGET – H WING

*IN A CLASS OF TEN GIRLS IN LOW NEWTON, I ASKED HOW MANY HAD BEEN PUT INTO CARE AS CHILDREN, OR WHOSE PARENTS MARRIAGE HAD BROKEN UP INVOLVING THEM IN SEPERATION.*
*SEVEN OUT OF THE TEN GIRLS RAISED THEIR HANDS.*

# Remembering Home

*T.H.*

My house was up a big steep hill from the town. It looked lonely, and plain, as the big family I had grown up with had all left. It had a big spikey fence around it, and a dog that barked all day. The town was very quiet during the week, but Saturday brought everyone out to shop.

I would climb to the top of the hills that surrounded my house, and down the other side to the foot of Ben Nevis, climbing up the steep rocky hillside, to the shoulder of the Ben, passing waterfalls, and crossing the aluminium bridges, that looked out of place.

When you think you have reached the top, you have another hill to go. You feel as though you are on top of the world, on a cloud, and when you look over the side you see more clouds, and the little dots that are homes. You feel proud that you have climbed the highest mountain in Britain, and it is so peaceful, and quiet, you could scream, and no-one would hear you, and you could end your life in one second, with the snow covering empty gaps, where you might go through a drop of 50,000 feet.

You then climb down, and you feel unimportant and you start getting smaller, and you reach the bottom, leaving all the peacefulness behind, where it belongs, going back to where you belong.

Aged eighteen.

## Angela Barker – LOW NEWTON

*Sunday*
*March 18/85*

*Dear S.A.S. 'H' Wing Durham,*

*I like your poems very much. They are sensitive, and emotional, and what I would expect having heard your lively and stimulating contributions to our Tuesday evenings.*

*You have a love of words, and handle them with affection, and the spirit of what you intend shines clearly through.*

*What I would suggest to you however, is to get your first draft of a poem down, and then ruthlessly apply yourself to pruning it, and polishing it, until it shines like a gem. A passion for words very often gets in the way of a precise, and literal meaning.*

*To this end, I have done an exercise in cutting your first poem Doubt. You may think it drastic, but if it achieves the same end, nothing has been lost, but excess.*

**What do you think?**

| *Original version* | *Suggestions* |
|---|---|
| *Am I myself now, is this really me?* | *Am I myself?* |
| *Have I become another self,* | *Have I become another,* |
| *I walk, and talk in the same way as* | *So altered,* |
| *I did before this time.* | *Though I walk, and talk* |
| *Can an environment alter us so* | *the same,* |
| *drastically,* | *My past eradicated,* |
| *That we eradicate our past* | *Moving sideways into* |
| *selves,* | *shadow,* |
| *And move sideways into shadows.* | |

17

Are we but mere actresses upon a
                        stage,
And take on that cloak of time,
Not out of choice, but necessity
            of our surroundings,
To be a heap of twigs in a forest,
A bridge in the middle of the ocean,
Would that be explicable?
The twigs covered by falling leaves,
The bridge encased by waves,
Not seen now as what they were,
For they have become part of
            where they are.

An actress,
Cloaked by time's
            necessity.


A heap of twigs,
An ocean bridge,

The one covered by
            leaves,
The other by waves.
Inexplicable!
No longer seen,
Merely part of where
            they are.


118 words

55 words


*I have not added any words of my own, only used your words, and as you see the reduction is over fifty per cent. I believe this is what all the best poets do, even when it really hurts to throw away the words you are in love with. It makes it more accessible.*

*By the way I am reminded that any written work submitted to me must be left to be read by those in charge, before I take it away.*

*It is incumbent upon me to go along with this, but I wouldn't willingly breach your confidentiality. I thought it best to let you know.*

Regards, Tom

# With Open Hands

Silence is night
And just as there are nights
With no moon
And no stars
When you are alone.
Totally alone.
When you are cursed
When you become a nothing which no one needs
So there are silences

Which are threatening, because there is nothing
Except the silence
There can be nothing – except silence.

Even if you open your ears, and your eyes
It keeps going on.
Without hope or relief.
Night with no light
No hope
I am alone in my guilt
Without forgiveness
Without love
Then desperately I go looking for friends
Then I walk the streets – a body
A sigh
A sound – for nothing.

But there are also nights with stars
With a full moon
With the light from a house in the distance
And silences which are peaceful and reflective
The noise of a sparrow in a large empty church
When my heart wants to sing out with joy.
When I feel that I'm not alone
When I'm expecting friends
Or remember nothing
I am alone
A body
A sigh
A sound – for nothing

### Julie Middleton – H WING DURHAM

# Graffiti

Geordie boys don't fuck about,
They do their bird, and get straight out.

### Anon. – LOW NEWTON

# A Normal Day

The alarm bell sounds in the morning light,
I look out the window, and the stars are bright,
It's sunny outside, the rain comes down, ·
I'll forget my umbrella, before I get to town,
I spotted a cat killing a mouse,
The birds are barking on top of the house,
The dead cat screamed as it ran by,
The sycamore grew an apple pie,
People were running, dogs were walking,
The flying pig laughed, and started talking.

Twenty four hours gone, I'll go for a cuppa,
I might even get back in time for supper.

**A Sixsmith – LOW NEWTON**


# Doledrums

Dole, unemployed,
Why can't we have a job,
The youth are people,
But the old don't care,
They say we're thugs, and morons,
lBut they're the mugs,
'Cos we're the people who come after them,
And can change their lives,
So why don't they give us a chance,
I mean to say, we have got brains,
Maggie Thatcher doesn't give a monkeys,
She's alright, she gets paid,
While the unemployed goes up, and up.
So, come on Maggie, be a bit mad,
And give us a bloody job.

**David J. Dunkin – LOW NEWTON**

ka Liisa Konttinen

*"Where's Stacey?"*
"Rule 43!" they explained.

I missed him, and all his six foot four, of dread-locked, smiling, West Indian exuberance. Childlike, and engaging, he was popular with the 'cons' in an indulgent way, in that they seemed to think of him as a being without menace. Whatever mean, cruel, shadowy world of gangsterdom he'd matured in, it had never destroyed his natural good humour.

But when you can't pay back what you've borrowed from the money barons of 'Frankland', you've just got to take your charm into splendid isolation.

T.H.

# Night Nurse

Tell her come, make it quick,
I am really very sick,
Tell her it's emergency,
Patient, name of Gregory,
No prescription here for me,
She's my cure, my remedy,
I don't need to see no Doc,
Need a nurse, love me round the clock,
Tell her only she will do,
Because my heart is broke in two.

Night nurse, only you can quench my thirst,
Night nurse, the pain is getting worse.

### Stacey Miller – FRANKLAND

# In a Rut

In a state, can't concentrate,
Won't give in, can't love, or hate.

I don't want you to relate,
Just go, and leave me to my fate,

22

I'm in a rut got to get out.

You think I'm dim,
You should've listed when your mother
Said, 'No good come of him'

Well, for you I don't feel nothing,
Some you lose, some you win,
Alright! so I'm no King,
But remember one thing.

I'm in a rut,
And I'm going to get out of it.

**Stacey Miller – FRANKLAND**

# Cell D.2. 35

The cell window boasts its mottled iron
bars, protecting societys entirety.

Perspiring walls emit their odours
Through a decade's **graffiti**.
And I spend the night embracing despair.

The floor kept company by melancholy
shuffling feet, has a defeated look.
And the door, observer of a thousand nights
despair, it's indentations write a book,
kissing, caressing, her long black hair.

Lying on the bed, and mattress,
That has known more men than a whore,
I listen to the guard roam the jail,
knowing all is safe and secure,
And I spend the night embracing despair.

My ceiling, mirror of all those wonderful
dreams, draws, and welcomes me back,
For all prison's decaying oppression,
Of dreams, and memorys there is no lack,
Kissing, caressing her long black hair,

And I spend the night embracing despair,
Kissing, caressing, her long black hair.

### Colin Blackshaw – DURHAM JAIL

The first thing you notice in prison, after the smell, there is no such thing as a new day.

### Melvyn – DURHAM

We hated this P.T.I., and we were playing Murder Ball.
"Righto lads", he says, "When I blow this whistle you can all settle your grievances,
and no-one will be put on report."
He blew, and twenty lads fell on him.

### Don't Quote Me – DURHAM

So I goes to see the psycho, and he says, "Why is it you answer every question, with
another question?"
And I says, "Who? Me?"

### Danny Boy – DURHAM JAIL

*"So, what's it really like dad?"*
*"Inside! Can't say, just visiting doesn't tell you very much"*
*"Must have some idea, by now!"*
    *"Well. Take our little bedroom! If I pushed you inside, locked the door, and said,
'You are not coming out until this time tomorrow, right!"*
    *"Right!"*

24

*"After ten mintues you'd be shouting, 'O.K. dad I get the message! After one hour, you'd be shouting, 'if this is some kind of a joke, I don't think it's very funny'. After ten hours, you'd be banging on the door, and calling me worse than Ian Macgregor.*

*If at that point, I opened the door, not to let you out, but pushed in this man who'd cut up his mother-in-law, and this stranger squatted down, and had a shit in a potty in front of you. Then afraid of whatever else he might do, you had to spend the rest of the night with his stink, and his company, until I let you out next day, you'd never speak to me again.*

*That is a bit what it's like, except that in your case it would only be for 24 hours your mother would be downstairs, the bedroom is warm, comfortable, and familiar, the window is not barred, and people would feel very sorry for you, and wonder how any father could treat a son in such a manner."*

T.H.

# Twenty Minutes on a Sunday Morning

"It's bloody freezin' in here".

"I know", he said.

"There'll be no exercise either, with this snow, we'll be stuck in this Pokey bleedin' cell all day".

"Do you want a game of cards John?"

"Naw it's too f'n cold".

I lie with my head under the blankets, so as not to waste the heat from my breath.

"Who do you vote for John?"

"I don't vote"

This reply always gets me angry, I always ask any different cell mate the same question, and I always get the same reply.

"Why not?"

"Duno, I jus' never bother".

I'm not sure if my anger is not really directed at myself, because I've never voted either. I've always been inside.

"F.n. apathy, that's what it is John".

"Y'reckon".

"Do you know what either of the major parties, stands for?"

"Not really! One's for the rich, an' the other's for the poor, i'sn it"

"Sommat like that".

The bloody idiot, I suppose all he does outside is get by on his dole, and spend hours half asleep in front of a television set, absorbing all that shit and propaganda.

"I read novels as well".

"Who? Mickey Spillane?"

"Yea! he's alright".

Well, if all us working class gets like him, the f.n. conservatives will be sterilising us while we are watching the tele, 'cos they say we only breed criminals anyway.

25

"The pidgeons are shouting you on the window ledge
Tony, are you gonna feed them?"
"What! after that screw threatened to nick me for encouragin' them! Course I am".
"Poor little bastards will be starving".
"Gorra load o' bread here, I collected off the trays this mornin'"
They've been like little friends, and pleasant distractions during the past nine months, and I feel I owe them.
"Anyway, if the sod nicks me, I'll write to the Animal Liberation Front, the papers, the lot. Can you see that then John? 'Man Penalised for Feeding Birds During Bleak Snowy Weather'"
They're God's creatures too. Man thinks he is so bloody superior. Everything else is second rate, or vermin. Matter of bloody opinion, I say.
"Christ, I'm pissed off John. I'm bored to tears. Oh' I'm startin' to think about friggin' women again. I think I'll try an' write a story, like that Tom Hadaway."

### T. Mills – DURHAM JAIL

# One in a Million

Don't ask what makes me do it.
What makes me be this way.
These girls they come to prison,
They're all a sudden gay.

they tell me that they love me,
They tell me that they care,
They promise love for ever,
In the end they leave me bare.

Though one leaves there's always another,
No matter how I try,
I say to myself, don't get involved.
They only make you cry.

But there'll always be another,
For a while I can say is mine,
'Cause when I'm really honest,
It's how I do my time.

### Laura Greenwood – H WING

26

# Extract

I sensed that the balance between us lay upon a complicated framework of strategies. She would try desperately to make me jealous with her little amours out on the wing, and I would deliberately ignore them. Then she would goad me into an argument, and then for an hour or so we would hurl insults at each other across the table, snapping and spattering the words like shrapnel. The others had to contend with all this, but were really very tolerant. Ignoring our histrionics, patiently listening, while each grumbled about the other, to whichever hapless individual had been chosen. The arguments were heated, but always with a deep unshakeable affection. When one lives with a partner in close proximity, twenty four hours out of everyday, a safety valve is necessary.

## Marian Coward – LOW NEWTON

*You can meet all sorts in prison. Like, the Bishop of Durham came in one day, and I said,*

*"Do you think you get steered around, making sure you only see what they want you to see?"*

*He has this slight, hesitant way of cupping a hand to his ear, as if you are not speaking clearly, or he is slightly deaf.*

*"I think so! I think so! But there are other ways of gaining a real impression".*

*Earlier I'd watched him cross the compound in company with the Governor, and floating down from the cell windows, the strident, but disembodied voices of the inmates opinionated the dubious parentage of prison officers. I don't think he can be all that hard of hearing.*

*T.H.*

# Wild Wind

The wind is wild,
It frightens me.
The wind is free,
It carries me.

It takes me high above the walls,
To the deep darkness of the moors.
It sets me down so gently.
On grass, that bends to its majesty.

It swirls about my feet
As if to clothe me in its cloak
And brings me scents so sweet
I feel this moment should not be broke.

Its gusts grip me around the waist
Like hands that are large
Yet, gently they bid me haste
For the wind must move, that's its charge.

It takes me along
to places far and wild
always whistling a mournful song.
Each time settling me down like a frail child.

But then it dies, and all is calm.
And I find
I am in the arms,
Of the one I left behind.

In my dreams,
Of the wild wind,
It was as no other dream,
For who can feel the caress of a wild wind.

*AND NOT FEEL FREE*

**C. Hickman – H WING**

# Stay Free to a Friend

We met at school,
Took no shit, played it cool,
Teachers said, we were dumb,
When we pick on everyone,

Wanting Saturday night to come,
Get a girl, have some fun.
Sometimes you want to be alone,
Lock the door to your room,
While I go on a nicking spree,
I hit wrong, I got three.
You write to ask are the screws too tight,
But you still keep me feeling bright.

Years pass, and I will change, and go,
Anywhere I want to blow,
And if you in the pub tonight, have a drink on me,
But go easy, step lightly, stay free.

**Stacey Miller – FRANKLAND**

# Drugs 3

I'm your Mammy, I'm your Daddy,
I'm that nigger in the alley,
I'm your doctor when you need,
Want some coke? Have some weed!
You know me, I'm your friend,
I'm your main line to the end,
I'm the pusher man!

It sure is kind of funny,
How the man takes your money,
He's as sweet as he can be,
To help you lose reality,
You can't reason with the pusher man,
Finance is all he understand.

Be glad to have your own,
I hope that you will see,
Lifes a high,
The man can't push his drugs on me!

**Stacey Miller – FRANKLAND**

29

*He just poked his head in the door, and asked what was going on, so I gave him Atyia's poem. Well I thought it was a well written piece, and to have been achieved with such spontaneity following our discussion on justice. After he'd gone, they grinned, and said, 'That was a visiting magistrate'.*

*T.H.*

# Judgement

Within these four walls, I sit looking out
       at the courtyard
Graveyard more like.
The wind whips round like a fierce lion.
Roaring, and whimpering,
Picking up the candy wrapper,
Sending it dizzy.
Then setting it down again,

Playing games, rather like the judges,

Up-down,
Up-down,
You either fly off over the fence,

Or you are discarded, like a piece of rubbish,

In the bin.

## Atyia Wilson – LOW NEWTON

"Low Newton! Breedin' ground for Frankland. He shouldn't be here for a start."
*The prison officer pointed out the seventeen year old, shuffling along on exercise. In the circling column of boys, he looked head down, isolated, bewildered.*
"On remand for medical report, y'know. Could be here weeks. The' don't know where else to send them. Likes o' him, should be in hospital. Bloody magistrates!"
*None of my business, or was it?*
*Sadness, and anger arises out of being aware that whatever brought them here, their continuing experience merely reinforces the chaos.*

*T.H.*

# The Fight

"Keep to the right, single file, keep your f'n mouths shut".
We enter the dining hall, pick up our trays. Halfway thro' porridge, two lads start arguing.
"Where's my bread gone?"
"I dunno. What you askin' me for?"
"I put three pieces there, and they are gone".
"You tryin' to say I took 'em?"
"Yeh! I am".
"Yeh' What ye gonna do about it?"
The first boy looked frightened. He didn't want to fight, but to back down now would lose respect in front of everyone. Building up his courage, he said.
"I'll punch your f'n head in"
The second boy said,
"Right! I'll see you in the gym".
News of the fight passed thro' the prison. In the changing room the two lads sat facing each other from opposite ends of the room, each with their own group of supporters. The second lad came over, started pushing the first lad.
"Come on then, punch my head in".
Tears were forming in the first lad's eyes. I could see he didn't want to fight. I stepped forward.
"Leave him alone, can't you see he don't want to fight".
A couple of lads turned on me.
"Keep out of it".
I stepped back.
"Come on then you shit".
The first lad swung wildly with his fist, and let out a little scream. The second lad absorbed the blow, and started raining blows back. Just at that moment the door opened, and the gym screw put his head round. I thought, good, now it will be stopped. I was wrong. Seeing the fight, he turned round, and went out. I can't help but remember the smaller lad getting beaten to the ground.
I am eighteen years old.

## No. 393 – LOW NEWTON

# Yesterday

Yesterday in the dining room, someone threw something over the tables, and hit me on my back. I shouted "Who the f'n hell was that?" Everyone stared at me. I ignored them. As I was going back to my pad a f'n screw pushed me out the way.
I had a piss. That's better! Sat on my bunk, and had a fag. My pad mate argued with

me, 'cos he'd nicked all my baccy. I fell asleep. Next day my pad mate said,
"Yor towel is dry".
'Cos he was licking up to me. I ignored him, the shit. Before dinner my social worker
come, and said,
"Yor mother does not want you home anymore".
I said, "So shit! I don't give two . . .".
She said I was going to get community service when I got to Crown Court, and where
was I going to live?
I said, "I don't f'n know".
I started banging my head of the wall, and was shouting,
"The f'n bitch, the cow! she never cared about me"
I went back to me cell, and started to take it out on my cell mate. Everytime he
opened his mouth I told him to piss off.
Then I sat down, and thought about it, and I apologised to my cell mate, got a wash,
and went to bed.
I am eighteen years old.

## No. 697 – LOW NEWTON

# Back Again

Coming from Crown Court in the paddy wagon, locked up like an animal.
A two foot by eight foot cage, freezing cold. Colder than a fridge. Then you get
here, Low Newton Remand Centre. Wow! big deal!

"Back again, 702"
"Aye sir!"
"What for this time?"
"T.W.O.C."
"When did you get out?"
"March eighteenth"
"Last year?"
"No, this. Got set up this time, black..."
"Aye' 702, they all say that".
"What's the point of talkin' to you's. You's don't care a monkeys..."
"Shut you mouth son, and call me sir"
"Why should I?"
"'Cos if you don't I'll put you down the block".
"Oh' you scare me! You forget I've been here before".
"Aye! too many times son".

'"So what's it got to do with you's?"
"Just one thing 702. You help me stay in a job".

I am nineteen years old.

## No. 702 – LOW NEWTON

# MONICA

There is this kid Monica! She's black. Are you taping this, 'bloody hell'.

Well she's about nineteen, didn't know how to write, speaking very badly, and seems below average intelligence. She is very big, but really gentle.

She kept driving everybody mad, because she wanted you to talk to her. She'd be in a cell with you, and it was like this Monica would start saying,

"Do you like me?" "Do you really like me?" "Tell me if you like me" "You like to be in a cell with me, don't you?"

After a day or so people get very fed up with this.

"Please Monica, get out of my cell before I kill you"...

She couldn't do anything for herself. She'd come in for kicking a window. That's how she went on. Kicking a window,come in for two three months, go to Styal, go off, a day later kick another window.

I was in Risley eleven months, and she came in four times.....

Finally she decided to go in for big crime. Diving over the counter of Marks and Spencers, pinched the money out of the 'till, then going to this rail of clothes, she crouched down, and hid behind it, the money in her hand, waiting for the coppers to come.

When she came back to Risley, she was saying "oh! I'll get nine months now, I can go and see my friend there".

This friend was an   officer! She related to officers, and prison life you know. She made mothers, and aunties out of them. She'd come, and say "Oh! hello, Mrs. so, and so, I'm back now you see. I came back".

# Help

## Menna – H WING, DURHAM

She was ill. I mean, really ill, and no one was taking a blind bit of notice.

Got no sympathy from us, I can tell you. So, what can you expect, we've got us bird to do. I mean, stone me, I've got twenty, thirty years to get thro', without coping with desperately sick people. There she went on, and I mean really went on, "I'm gonna kill meself, I'm gonna kill meself". I'm talking about every every night when we're trying to get some sleep, y'know.

Well, she's drugged up all day, they're pumping her full of drugs, but she's coming out of them at night just when the rest of us are turning in.

33

"I want to die, I want to die".

She's in the strips y'know. A smock, a mattrass on the flor, and no way she can harm herself.

"If ye don't let me out of here, I'm counting up to ten, and then I'm gonna kill myself."

I mean, night after night, for God's sake, let her get on with it.

Count to ten! We all started shouting back, ten, nine, eight, seven, six...y'know.

If we could have thought of a way to help her, believe me, we would. Yes! I mean help her top herself!

Anyhow, she got this idea herself. She's looking at the alarm button, and thinking, 'if I pick away at the cement, and plaster, I'll be able to get at the flex, pull some out, and hang meself'. So she's picking away, and it works, she pulls a little piece of flex, then a bit more, and then some more until she's got enough to wrap round her neck.

So, with it firmly wrapped round her neck, she shouts 'goodbye everybody', 'good bye world', and flops violently onto the floor. What happens! Another bloody two yards of flex, comes out the wall, doesn't it. So, she picks herself up, and desperately charges across the cell, hoping she'll garrot herself on the way. More bloody flex comes out. The cell is festooned with it. What's more all the bloody alarms bells are ringing all over the wing. 'Screws' are dashing round, reassuring everyone. Looking in the spy holes! 'Fault on the system Judy, don't worry'. 'Everything alright Penny, don't get upset'. 'Till they come to the strip cell, and look in, 'Nothing to worry about Mary,... oh' my God!'

There she is sitting in the middle of all this wiring, and she's laughing. Yes laughing! The situation struck her as being so funny, she gave up any thought of killing herself. She was cured.

## Judith Ward – H WING, DURHAM

*The prison officer was showing me a typical cell in this restricted area as part of my introduction.*

*The inmate was an enormous bearded man.*

"Just showing him you cell", said the officer.

"It's no ma fucking cell, it's your fucking cell, an' you can have the fucking thing back as soon as ye fucking like".

*I felt I was just an in between. I looked around, the officer was standing behind me. I was an in between. I apologised, and left.*

*T.H.*

7.3 85,

yesterday When the man cam to see us
I fort it Wos very intaresting When
I Went bac to my pad I had a
very good think about it Well When I Was
laid in my pad the sun Wos shining
in my Window and it made my think
about all the things out side I should be
out side With my son and my geirlfriend.
I am missing out on a Lot of thing
I Wish I Wos out so I could be out
and make A new Life.

35

Northumbria ........Police     Newcastle 'B' .....Division     Gosforth. ......Station

Previous convictions in respect of ▮▮▮▮▮▮▮▮▮▮▮▮▮▮▮▮▮ ..........    C.R.O. No.............

| SENTENCE | COURT | DATE | OFFENCE AGE | Release Date |
|---|---|---|---|---|
| Prob. Order 2 yrs | Newcastle Juvenile | 3.5.61 | Larceny. 9½ | Age ~~~~ |
| Con. Disch. 12 mths ✗ | Newcastle Juvenile | 21.2.62 | Housebreaking. 10 | ~~~~ |
| Comm. to care of L.A. | Newcastle Juvenile | 4.4.62 | Larceny 2 cases 10 ( cases tic). | ~~~~ |
| Comm to Axwell Park App. School. | Whitley Bay Juv. | 25.6.64 | Shopbreaking. 12¼ Larceny 2 cases (17 cases tic). | ~~~~ |
| App. School Order. | Newcastle Juvenile | 23.6.65 | Housebreaking 13½ Larceny (3 housebreaking 1 storebreaking tic). | |
| Returned to App. School | Whitehaven Co. Juv. | 24.6.66 | Housebreaking 14½ Larceny (2 tic's). | |
| Placed in care of L.A Abs. Disch. ✗ | Newcastle Juvenile | 17.7.68 | Shopbreaking. 16¼ Att. shopbreaking. | |
| Con. Disch. 1 2 mths. ✗ | Newcastle Juvenile | 28.8.68 | Shopbreaking. 16½ | |
| Prob. Order 3 yrs. Fined £35 No action | Northumberland Q.Sess | 11.7.69 | Burglary. 17½ Burglary. Re br. of Con. Disch. 28.8.68. (1 burglary 1 Att. TWOC tic). | |
| Borstal Training on each Con. Disch. 1 yr. disq. 1 yr. Borstal Training conc. | Northumberland Q. Sess | 19.9.69 | Burglary 2 cases 18 A/Abet no insurance. Br. of P.O 11.7.69 (9 TWOC 3 Burglary 2 theft tic). | |
| Borstal Training each | BORSTAL Recall 6ᵀᴴ Northumberland Q. Sess. | 17.9.70 | Burglary 2 cases. Theft. 19 TWOC (4 burglary 1 TWOC 1 Att. TWOC tic). | |
| (RELEASED ON HOME LEAVE 4.6.70 — 10.6.70 TO 150 DORRINGTON RD. | | | | |
| New Order Borstal Trng. (REASED ON PAROLE FROM WETHERBY 2.12.71 — 2.2.71) | Northumberland Q. Sess | 23.3.71 | Going equipped - theft. 19½ Burglary 2 cases. 20 | |
| 3 years Probation | Gosforth Magistrates | 9.2.72 | Burglary. 20 | |
| 6 mths impt. conc. 3 mths impt. conc. | Newcastle Crown | 27.3.72 | Burglary & TWOC. 20 Br. of P.O 9.2.72. (3 att. burglary tic) | |

Denotes "spent" conviction

L.D 33 ( RELEASED ON LICENCE & H/a 56 BROTHERLEE RD. HAYDON — LICENCE EXPIRES 15.6.73 )

| SENTENCE | COURT | DATE | OFFENCE | Dí |
|---|---|---|---|---|
| | | | | AGE |
| 12 mths impt. on each conc. No action taken | Newcastle Crown | 31.10.72 | Burglary 2 cases. Re Prob.Order 9.2.72. (3 burglary 1 Obt. by dec. tic). | 21 |
| 9 mths impt. susp. 2 yrs. Sup. Order 12 mths | Newcastle Crown | 17.9.73 | Burglary. (1 burglary tic). | 22 |
| 9 mths impt. on each conc. | Newcastle Crown | 4.2.75 | Burglary 2 cases. Br. of S/Sent 17.9.73. | 23 |
| 6 mths impt. conc. to 4.2.75. | Newcastle Crown | 24.3.75 | Burglary. | 23 |
| 3 mths impt. 7 days impt. conc. L.E. | Newcastle Crown | 17.11.75 | Burglary. T.W.O.C. | 24 |
| 9 mths impt. 15 mths impt. on each. conc. | Newcastle Crown | 26.4.76 | Theft. Burglary. | 24 |
| | | | | 25½ |
| 6 mths impt. | North Shields Mags. | 13.5.77 | Theft. | |
| 2 yrs impt. 18 mths impt. on each. conc. | Newcastle Crown | 10.7.78 | Burglary. Burglary 2 cases. Att. burglary. (6 burglary 2 theft tic). | 26½ |
| ( HOME LEAVE FROM HM.P. KIRKHAM 24.7.79 - 30.7.79 c/o 120 KIRKWOOD DR., N/KRUTON ) | | | | |
| 3 yrs impt. on each conc. | Newcastle Crown | 18.2.80 | Burglary 2 cases. | 28 |
| ( RELEASED - PAROLE -18.2.81 - 27.11.81 - CANCELLED 6.8.81 ) | | | | |
| 3 years impt. on each conc. 3 years impt. conc. | Newcastle Crown | 6.8.81 | Burglary 3 cases. Att burglary | 29½ |
| adj. (BAIL) 28 dys Bas Roster assessment | Newcastle Crown | 5.12.83 | Burglary Burglary | 32 |
| Bench Warrant | " | 3.1.84 | Failed to abbear | 32 |
| 5 yrs imh. (Extended Sent.) 15 mths. imh. concurrent 2 mths imh. concurrent | " | 25.5.84 | Burglary - House Burglary - shoh Breach of Bail 1 t.i.c. | 32½ |

? Could all this be a excuse. A form of away out foe my self from problems . An I in seculee.

# Lord Nelson

Alone amidst the apprehensive crowd,
the solitary clown screams,
Nurses in erotic white coats,
assure him, "It's only a dream".

Alice plays in wonderland,
vest blotting the urine pool.
The pencil fits in Hare's eye,
punishment! Hare plays it cool.

Adolf's cut her throat, Adolfs cut her
throat, hear the melodic chant
as hygienic coats hurtle past,
to save another confident.

And I, standing on my bridge,
captain of this mighty ship,
supposed to win this bloody war
with an unpatriotic crew, of lunatics.

### Colin Blackshaw – DURHAM

*Written while in solitary confinement _ Hull Prison.*

# Life

You thought your life sweet, so now let's meet,
And take a trip through time,
I'll show you a room, in a place of gloom,
And shatter your dreams sublime.

Where cruel 'cards' tell a story
On one-eyed doors of steel,
And a thousand names, and numbers,
Feel a hate which makes you reel.

'a' speaks of aggression,
'E' of desperate flight,
There's a stink of foul repression,
And endless years in sight.

The 'cards' spell hope with a number,
Despair if it rises high,
But the 'card' that has no number,
Four letters curse the eye.

Release your tears, I can see your fears,
And well you might feel dread,
'Life' now for you, is something new,
It's the mark of the living dead.

**Peter Humble – FRANKLAND**


# Night Talk

Oh' my mate come in from Newcastle last night. He's a good mate of mine. You should've heard me laugh with joy. I could not believe who it was, but sure enough it was him, my drinking partner on the out.

I started to shout, not very loud, but loud enough.

"What you in for Stew?"
"Oh' just for robbery. What you in for?"
"Oh' two house burglaries, what you expecting?"
"About eighteen months".
"I'm expecting two years"
"well Stew, we'll be out soon".

I listened for a bit, I could hear the shuffle of paper.

"Stew! Stew! what ye doing Stew?"
"Hold on man, I'm on the bog".
"Hurry up Stew, lights out soon".

**P. Borrowdale – LOW NEWTON**

# Xmas Day

We woke early on Xmas Day, but we were not very excited. No one was very cheerful, it wasn't a bright day. The screw opened my cell door to slop out, I wasn't bothered. I wasn't expecting any presents or nice surprises. I knew there would be no party, although a few greetings wouldn't have come amiss. I hadn't had any visits, no one seemed to care. I went back to me cell, and laid on my bunk.

There was something missing. I stared aimlessly at the stone gray walls, and steel door. There was no Xmas tree, no bright coloured lights, or gay decorations, such as I'd always known as a child.

I turned over, trying to disregard my bleak surroundings, and tried to sleep, until I would be woken at 11.45 for dinner. Xmas inside.

**Askey – LOW NEWTON**
Aged 17

*FOOTNOTE*

| | |
|---|---|
| Governor. | *"At Xmas we had decorations in the main hall, and Xmas trees in every passageway. Every prisoner was given a cigar."* |
| Remedial Two. | *"The walls isn't gray anyhow, and Askey always was a moaner."* |
| T.H. | *"If gray is how you feel, gray is how it looks. And he is only seventeen.* |

*T.H.*

# If I Don't Speak

If I don't speak,
    Then people won't ask me things,
And I won't have to lie,
    It's a good way you see,
I upset no-one at all,
    They try, and make me talk,
Someone will sit holding a daffodil,
    And say, 'Ful-low-er'

40

`Over, and over again.
    This is fun,
They try to catch me out too,
    "Do you want a sweet?"
But I just take it,
Smiling at their stupidity.
I like being quiet, no-one else does.
    They chitter chatter around me.
I wonder how they hear, or understand,
    I hear lots,
One day I might speak,
    Shock them all,
Then, they would be quiet,
    And I would laugh,
And never say, another word.

**David – FRANKLAND**

# Secrets

My grandfather ate onions,
Pickled ones,
By the jar,
He would sit, and crunch, and munch.
And chew them.
My grandmother introduced,
Onion prohibition;
My grandfather went underground,
Often, I would keep watch,
And share his pleasure,
But not his onions,
Sometimes, he would pat me on the head,
With yellow stained fingers,
Pungent with the tell tale odour,
I secretly enjoyed this,
It was my rebellion,
If my mother knew, she'd fume,

Like the onions.
Now he's gone,
I can never pass an onion jar,
Without smiling,
People think that's strange,
But me, and my grandfather,
Keep our secrets.

David – FRANKLAND

*This concentration of so many tragic lives under the one roof is disturbing.*

*T.H.*

# Broadmoor

"Remember the time, the bastards sent me to Broadmoor, I was only twenty one."
"What did they do that for Millsy?"
"'Cos I battered a screw. Treating me like I was a turd or somethin'. I think the place might have got to me, if I hadn't been so young, and had a sense of humour.
I remember one old wrinkled prune, who asked me for a game of draughts."
"But I warn you", he said, "I haven't been beat for 70 years".
"O.K.", I said, to humour the old buggar.
"I always have red" he said.
"O.K. by me", so I made a move. The old fellow pushed it back, so I thought he wanted to move first, so I waited. Then he said, "You move first". So I moved again. Then he pushed it back. This went on a couple of more times, so I said, "How we going to play, if we don't move?"
"At this he jumped up, and hit me on the chin, and stomped off. I just laughed it off.
Another time I went to the shithouse, and a guy was making weird noises in one of the cubicles, so I looked over as I passed, and there was this daft ...., standing there with a turd on his head, waving his arms, making this funny noise.
"What you doing mate??', I said.
"I'm down at the pub havin' a pint".
"Oh' aye".
"Yeh! it really works. You can transport yourself anywhere, through this shit on your napper".
One of the worst, was this guy I'd come in with from Manchester, called Greg. Seemed as sane as me, turned out the friggin' pottiest. He was put in the same ward, next

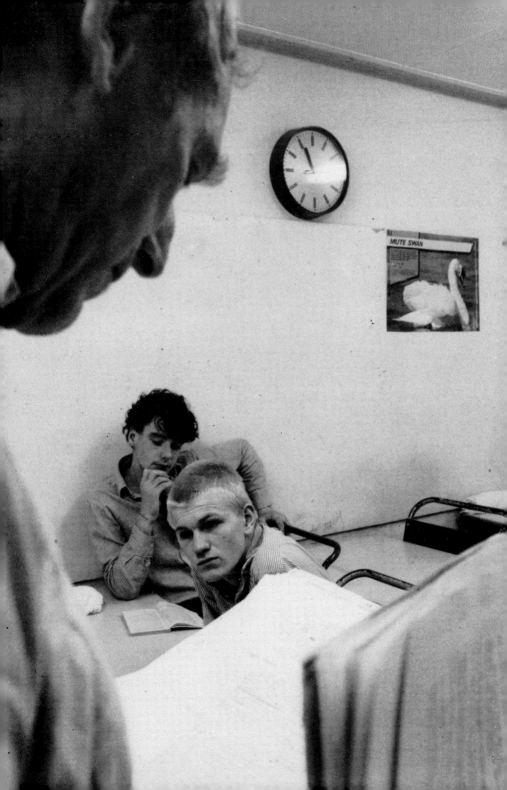

'bed to me. So I said, "This place is a bit dodgy eh! Did you see those friggin' cranks, up and down the ward last night?"

I'd woke up once, and one of them was staring at me, three inches from my boat race. Didn't get to sleep after that. So, I thought it would be safer, if we took it in turns to stay awake at nights. So we agreed, and he was on first, but he was on some sleeping drugs of some sort. So, I said, "When you get them tonight, keep them under your tongue, until you're out of sight, then I'll nick them".

So I gets me head down, and when I woke up next morning, I looked over to his bed, but it was empty. So, I'm going down for a wash, and this screw gives me a dirty look. So I said, "What's up with you?"

"You know what's up Mills".

Well I'm no friggin' mind reader, so how would I know.

"You told Gregson to batter up one of the other patients with a chair, and he's got a fractured skull."

"Oh' for f-'s sake". I didn't even bother denying it.

What a friggin' place this was.


I saw the psycho after about five months. He kept asking if I was queer. In the end I blew, and said, if he didn't stop going on about his latent homosexual tendencies, I'd rip his kecks off, and stuff it up his arse.

Anyway, I didn't see him for about another four months.

I think they were observing me.

When he called me up again, he said, he'd called me up to see if I was getting sane enough for release. So I said, what the f. you talkin' about? I'm doing' a set sentence of three years, I'm not here on your f'n say so."

"That's where your wrong Mills", he said. "I can keep you here as long as I want".

That was it for me. First chance I got, I was on the roof. I took a blanket with me, and for the first few hours, I threw a few slates down to keep up the tradition, then I climbed into one of the air vents on the roof, and put the blanket over the top to preserve the heat.


They ignored me for a few days.

"F'n psycho tactics Millsy". Yeh! I know. After about four days, they sent that stupid psycho out. He stood there with a big cigar, and a glass of whiskey in his hand. They really are jerks these people, they're crazier than the .... they lock up.

"That's true Millsy".

"Anyway, I shouted down that I thought he would look nice with a slate decoratin' his napper. That shifted the daft .....

When I came down, he had me in his office again, and he asked me why I shouldn't stay in Broadmoor for a little longer.

"Why?" "'Cos I'm not friggin' mad, that's why".

He was a weird ...., that ...., all he said, was "Oh' yes!" Anyway I got out not long after that.

"Yor right Millsy, it's a bit scary, to think they have all that power to shove us away, and label us mad etc."
"Yeh!"
"See ya later Tony".
"Yeh' see ya. Tirra".

## T. Mills – D WING, DURHAM

# Georgie Porgy

Georgie Porgy, pudding, and pie,
Starves the kids, and lets 'em die.

Georgie Porgy's got a Rolls,
The kids have got their empty bowls,

Georgie Porgy lives in style,
Kids in pain, can't raise a smile.

How come the world is so unfair,
Where people die, and we don't care.

Georgie Porgy, that's me and you,
Now tell me, what we're going to do.

## D.G. Beal – FRANKLAND

*A frequently expressed view of prisoners, was that they could never honestly write down their experience, and feelings, because it would be discovered by prison officers, and maybe used against them.*

*My own experience of uniformed staff, was of their circumspection, non-intrusive, and barely able to conceal their indifference.*

*In three areas it was incumbent upon me to 'hand in' for inspection any writing given to me, but nothing was ever censored, and I reminded prisoners of this condition, while assuring them that I would never willingly betray a confidence.*

*T.H.*
45

# Can I Have Me Batteries

Punishment in prison can be meted out for the slightest infraction of the rules, the system is based on tit-for-tat, which is the prison equivalent of justice, and fairness. If you're a naughty girl, we'll be naughty to you.

What, outside, would pass for ordinary emotional behaviour, is not tolerated. Excessive laughter, anger, frustration, even P.M.T. has to be controlled. The perfect prisoners are the clones, doing everything they're told, never raising their voices, losing their tempers, or horror of horrors, answering an officer back.

A few years ago, when work was short in the workroom, we spent the day sitting around gossiping.

This day, I was talking to two of my mates, and sitting cross-legged on the table. I'd been sat like that all morning, but come the afternoon, the officer who was icky (in charge) decided I should sit with a proper deportment.

"Get off that table!"

"What's wrong with you. I've been sat here all morning, it's comfortable."

"When I tell you to do something, do it, and don't answer back",

"Knickers!"

At this point my mates intervened, and pleaded with me to get off the table.

"No! I won't! Come an' get me off!"

"I won't tell you again, get off or you're on report."

Translated, this means, 'I am losing control of this situation, you are being nasty to me, so I am going to get your fags taken away from you'.

So yours truly gets off the table, and goes to collect a chair. As I reach the chair, I think, 'What am I doing?' 'I'm being a clone!' So I pick up the chair, and throw it across the room, where it bangs into a vacant machine. Having satisfied my anti-authority emotion, I go for a fag in the loo.

Five minutes later, the heavy mob arrive. Three great officers weighing at least forty stone between them, cart all seven stone of me off to my cell. The next day, report! Rather like a mini court, with the Gov, his body-guard, (male chief), our chief, the P.O. and two officers, with me stuck in between, trying to get a look see at the Gov.

They stand facing you, backs to the Gov., just in ase you decide you don't like your punishment, and that it's about time you gave the Gov a dig.

I always plead guilty, as I usually know beforehand I'm going to go on report, so I don't bother with all the fuss 'Not guilty' creates.

"Do you plead guilty or not guilty?"

"Guilty of course".

"Why did you throw the chair?"

"I felt like it. I think I'm a bit P.M.T."

"That's no excuse."

"It's not an excuse, just a fact. If I feel like throwing a chair I throw it."

"We can't have uncivilised behaviour. You will take 28 days loss of association, 28 days loss of privileges, and a £2.10p fine, and I suppose you think I'm a right bastard?"

"I do".

Liisa Konttinen

So, there I am, stuck behind the door for 28 days, no smokes, no radio, no association, no guitar, no bed until after ten, just what I needed! Well, I didn't mind the smokes, as your mates always keep you going, the radio it was that bothered me. No plays on Radio Four, no news, that's not punishment that's deprivation.

About a week later I remembered that the Chief in one of her 'I'll tell those cons what's what' moods, had put a list on the board of privileges, and entitlements, stating that you were entitled to a radio if you'd done more than eighteen months of your sentence. That was the mistake, a radio is a privilege, (which is wrong I think), not an entitlement. Well, next day the visiting magistrate came in on his weekly useless rounds. I collared him.

"I would like to have my radio".

"But it's a privilege, and you are on loss of privilege".

"If you go to the flat, you'll see a notice which states that radios are an entitlement when you've served eighteen months. Well I've served four years, and I want my radio."

The prison officer chipped in.

"That's a mistake".

"I know it's a mistake. You know it, he knows it, but it's there in black, and white, and I want my radio"

Next thing is the Gov arrives.

"Well, obviously it's a mistake. Call the Chief Officer".

"Sorry sir, it's a mistake. I'll take it down immediately".

"Well you see, it was a mistake", says God.

We call him God, because that's how he signs his name, Governor of Durham.

"I know it. You know it. Everyone knows it, but it's a mistake I didn't make, the notice is still on the board, and still in effect, and I want my radio".

Big conference outside the door. Door opens, Chief glares, red faced. God is smiling benignly. P.O. hands in my radio.

"Excuse me Guv, can I have my batteries out of the canteen, these are finished."

## Judith Ward – H WING, DURHAM

# Maria

There was a girl here in 'H' wing who hung herself. She was Hungarian, and had been here for several years.

She told us her husband was a pig, who beat her up, and gave her no money for food, so one day, unable to take any more, she decided to kill herself. Not wishing to leave her little boy, aged seven, behind, she gave him some sleeping tablets, then cut his throat. Then she took a hatchet, and tried to chop herself up, and then attempted to hang herself.

She survived, and regained consciousness in hospital, but her little boy was dead. She was given seven years.

She was a very quiet, polite woman, of about fifty years.

It was her boy's birthday one Saturday, and her husband sent her a little kid's birthday card with her son's name on it.

I think that must have been the last straw. She had been asking to see the shrink, but no-one took any notice of her.

She went to her room on Friday night, and hung herself. She put a cloth around her face so people wouldn't see it, and plugged up all her orifices. On Saturday morning we weren't unlocked. A 'screw' came round and told us she had 'died in the night'.

It was awful, we could hear them carrying her downstairs in a box. We were locked in until 11 am, then we went on exercise. It was unreal, everyone was so quiet.

Everyone liked Maria, and we really couldn't believe it. By teatime though everyone was back to normal.

## Penny .... – H WING, DURHAM

"Why write?"

*The tattooed, young man thrust his two weeks of assiduous scribbling into my hands, deprecating his own achievement.*

"It's no good, is it. I can't even spell?"

*I was compelled to admiration. He had done everything I had asked of him. In simple, unpretentious, but clear expression, he had added his own inner feelings to his remembered experience, and the momentum, and sheer exuberance of his words was enviable.*

*If he had come to the education block out of some desperate wish to redress the wasted years, that was not going to happen, but he had filled two exercise books cover to cover.*

*It was his story, but it could have been the story of any one of a thousand prisoners.*

*Removed from his mother, and family at the age of ten, and placed into 'care', by a magistrate who said,*

*"It's for your own good Billy!", pointing out that he had been out of control, and something had to be done.*

*But fifteen, and sixteen year old boys were in the same 'care', and they abused the ten year olds, so that 'for his own good', became a nightmare experience.*

*Well, you can't expect magistrates to know everything, but sometimes you wonder if education seperate some people from their imagination. Billy proceeded through*

49

*Remand homes, Children's homes, Borstals, Prisons, adding up to fifteen years of
sentencing out of his **thirty** three years of life.*

*Writing of being at the age of twelve, and coming home on leave from Egremont
Approved School, not having seen his family for a year, he remembers, ....*

*T.H.*

# The Homecoming. An Extract

Easter came round, how happy that made me. Mr. Jones got us up at four o'clock in
the morning, sixty of us, in our new clothes with white arm bands, and we marched in
twos, down to the bus stop at Egremont . . .

...., when we got in sight of Blaydon, I could see the chimney pots. Home, I thought,
and no police looking for me, even if it is only for a week. One never forget the feeling
inside of the sight of the place where you belong.

Newcastle was my home. I had a feeling of belonging, like that song. 'This is my
Country'. The joy of pulling into the terminus at the bottom of Fawden Road,
overwhelmned me. I wanted to run, and scream, this feeling of love was beyond belief.
All smartly dressed with my Italian suit, bag in my hand, and my head was up. I had not
seen my parents for a long time.

I walked unsteadily at first, afraid, looking around. This had become a different
world. Halfway to the flats, I saw my brother George. I shouted his name, "George!
George! He looked, and put his head down. He was talking to a smaller lad, and took no
notice of me. I got closer, and shouted again, 'George!' He stared, then all of a sudden
ran at me, "It's our Billy, our Billy!", and flew into my arms.

He was about six, or seven. The lad that was with him, I did not know, he was about
five, and moved up to me closely, and put his hand on my coat bottom.

George said, "It's our Chris, Billy!"

I put George down, and picked Chris up, and cuddled him. I was tongue tied.
"You're a big lad", I said, and off we went, me carrying him, and George running ahead
to tell our folks.

Before I got into the flat, I seen my Mum, and sisters at the window. I waved, and
they waved, and then I went into the Block. First thing I noticed, the coal sheds. Bad
memories there, I thought, and went up the stairs.

My mother had the door open. I stood. Our Florence was there, Elizabeth, my two

50

oldest sisters, then I seen a shy quiet girl, my youngest sister Margaret. She had grown lovely, long black hair, and there was our Stan.

"Hi' Billy!"

"Hi' Stan!"

It was so strange. I was strange, my family was strange, but there was love for each other, and the smiles were long. My Dad broke the ice.

"Lettim in! C'mon, lettim in".

## Billy – FRANKLAND

*Let him in indeed! Let him in!*

*T.H.*

**Billy – FRANKLAND**